NATURE

NATURE

Biblical TRUTHS

— *that* —

Celebrate Creation

B&H
PUBLISHING GROUP

NASHVILLE, TENNESSEE

CONTENTS

CONTENTS

There's a reason behind the term the great outdoors. There are so many things in this world that can leave us awestruck: the vastness of the ocean, the innumerable stars that only seem to be outnumbered by the grains of sand on a beach, the colors of a sunset, the burst of lightning. Whatever it may be, most of us have had a moment where stopping and smelling the roses turns into the observation of a world with countless infinitesimal features that only God could have created.

There's a reason that we go out for walks to clear our heads. It's simply because it is such a good and healthy thing for us to be out in God's creation. Some of us love that scenery so much that we even bring parts of it into our own home. Nature has a way to touch our souls in so many different ways that nothing manmade has ever been able to do.

God uses that creation to stir our hearts and use this creation to draw us closer to Him.

Think about your favorite place to go on vacation. Most of us probably say something along the lines of a place in nature. Some say their place is a cabin in the mountains, or a lake house, or a beach house. Some may talk about camping in the woods or a place where they can hike, but all of these have the same concept. We seek a place to "unplug." Most of us look for a place where we can be at peace. It only seems natural that the places that ease our hearts the most, are the places surrounded by God's creation.

"Therefore I tell you: Don't worry about your life, what you will eat or what you will drink; or about your body, what you will wear. Isn't life more than food and the body more than clothing? Consider the birds of the sky: They don't sow or reap or gather into barns, yet your heavenly Father feeds them. Aren't you worth more than they? Can any of you add one moment to his life-span by worrying?"

Matthew 6:25–27

———

Humble yourselves, therefore, under the mighty hand of God, so that he may exalt you at the proper time, casting all your cares on him, because he cares about you.

1 Peter 5:6–7

"Peace I leave with you. My peace I give to you. I do not give to you as the world gives. Don't let your heart be troubled or fearful."

    John 14:27

———

Don't worry about anything, but in everything, through prayer and petition with thanksgiving, present your requests to God. And the peace of God, which surpasses all understanding, will guard your hearts and minds in Christ Jesus.

    Philippians 4:6–7

———

For God has not given us a spirit of fear, but one of power, love, and sound judgment.

    2 Timothy 1:7

Father, ease my heart. I am anxious about different things going on in my life. I cannot rest, Lord, because I am constantly worried about what the next day will hold. Father, allow me to find peace. Allow me to find rest in You, Father. Thank You for caring for me, Lord. Amen

Most of us can think to ourselves about a place that has stopped us in our tracks. Some of us think about the tallest mountains. Some think about the ocean. Some of us even look up to the stars. What normally stops us is the knowledge of how small we really are in this world. It's not something that brings fear. Instead, it brings acknowledgement and respect. We acknowledge that there is something out there bigger than us. God holds such authority that He created the things in this world that make us realize our smallness in this great big world.

Then he said to them, "Give, then, to Caesar the things that are Caesar's, and to God the things that are God's." When they heard this, they were amazed. So they left him and went away.

Matthew 22:21–22

———

Jesus came near and said to them, "All authority has been given to me in heaven and on earth."

Matthew 28:18

———

Let everyone submit to the governing authorities, since there is no authority except from God, and the authorities that exist are instituted by God.

Romans 13:1

For this reason God highly exalted him and gave him the name that is above every name, so that at the name of Jesus every knee will bow—in heaven and on earth and under the earth—and every tongue will confess that Jesus Christ is Lord, to the glory of God the Father.

Philippians 2:9–11

———

Submit to every human authority because of the Lord, whether to the emperor as the supreme authority or to governors as those sent out by him to punish those who do what is evil and to praise those who do what is good. For it is God's will that you silence the ignorance of foolish people by doing good.

1 Peter 2:13–15

Lord, thank You for the mountains. Thank You for the ocean. Thank You for the stars. Thank You for having authority over all of the things of this world. Thank You for telling the tide to come no further. Thank You for knowing where every star is and where every grain of sand is placed. Father, thank You for loving me. For even in this vast universe of things only You understand, You still chose to love me. Amen

Beautiful doesn't even begin to describe what our world is. Think for a moment. Think about the moments that made you aware of the beauty in this world. Think of all the different hues in the sky as the sun rises and sets. Some of you may have been entranced by the different shades of green that each individual blade of grass comes together to form. Some of you may even find the blues and purples that follow a lightning strike to be mesmerizing. Whatever it may be, you have to admit . . . our God made a beautiful world.

I have asked one thing from the LORD;
it is what I desire:
to dwell in the house of the LORD
all the days of my life,
gazing on the beauty of the LORD
and seeking him in his temple.
    Psalm 27:4

———

I will praise you
because I have been remarkably and wondrously
made.
Your works are wondrous,
and I know this very well.
    Psalm 139:14

Charm is deceptive and beauty is fleeting,
but a woman who fears the LORD will be praised.
    Proverbs 31:30

———

You are absolutely beautiful, my darling;
there is no imperfection in you.
    Song of Songs 4:7

———

Don't let your beauty consist of outward things like
elaborate hairstyles and wearing gold jewelry, but
rather what is inside the heart—the imperishable
quality of a gentle and quiet spirit, which is of great
worth in God's sight.
    1 Peter 3:3–4

Heavenly Father, thank You for making this world. There are so many things that You've made happen that I can't even begin to imagine how they came to be. Father, allow me to look out into the world and recognize the beauty that You've created. Allow me to acknowledge the beauty of the things You made by simply speaking them into existence. Amen

Some people depend on the blessings that nature provides. Farmers pray for the right amount of rain and sunlight so their crops can thrive. Fishermen depend on calm seas to be able to effectively do their jobs. Even airlines are determined by the surrounding weather. God blesses so many each day through the softness of a breeze or the power of a rain storm. These things so often go unnoticed, but for some, these blessings can be the difference between success and failure.

"May the LORD *bless you and protect you; may the* LORD *make his face shine on you and be gracious to you; may the* LORD *look with favor on you and give you peace."*

Numbers 6:24–26

———

Indeed, we have all received grace upon grace from his fullness, for the law was given through Moses; grace and truth came through Jesus Christ.

John 1:16–17

———

And God is able to make every grace overflow to you, so that in every way, always having everything you need, you may excel in every good work.

2 Corinthians 9:8

Blessed is the God and Father of our Lord Jesus Christ, who has blessed us with every spiritual blessing in the heavens in Christ.

Ephesians 1:3

———

And my God will supply all your needs according to his riches in glory in Christ Jesus.

Philippians 4:19

Lord God, thank You for all that You do for me. I know there are so many times that I overlook what You have done in my life. Father, please continue to bless me. Thank You for loving me enough, Father, that You take care of me in ways that I don't even notice. Amen

You can tell a lot about a person in the way they tend a garden. There's a certain level of care and knowledge that is required for successful gardening. You have to think of the soil being used, the amount of water needed by each plant, which plants need a great deal of sunlight, and which plants only need a little. The same way we get to know the needs of each individual plant, God knows each and every one of our needs.

"I give you a new command: Love one another.
Just as I have loved you, you are also to love one
another. By this everyone will know that you are my
disciples, if you love one another."
    John 13:34–35

———

Carry one another's burdens; in this way you will
fulfill the law of Christ.
    Galatians 6:2

Therefore, as we have opportunity, let us work for the good of all, especially for those who belong to the household of faith.

   Galatians 6:10

———

Everyone should look out not only for his own interests, but also for the interests of others.

   Philippians 2:4

Heavenly Father, thank You for caring for me. Thank You for knowing all of my individual needs and meeting those needs. Lord, thank You for sustaining me. Allow me to go out into the world and care for those that need it. Instill in me a loving spirit to take care of those that are in need. Amen

In Asian communities, you sometimes hear stories of rice paddy farmers. It's a fascinating style of farming. Farmers will stand in puddles and move back inch by inch while placing seedlings in watery soil. They stand out in the sun all day and will have the sun bake their backs for hours on end, but something special will happen . . . a breeze. Whenever this light breeze hits, you see the farmers stand up and take the comfort of the breeze with gratitude—resting in that moment. When the breeze passes, they bend down and get back to work. How many little moments like this does God give us throughout the day? Do we act in gratitude of that comfort?

Even when I go through the darkest valley,
I fear no danger,
for you are with me;
your rod and your staff—they comfort me.
    Psalm 23:4

———

Remember your word to your servant;
you have given me hope through it.
This is my comfort in my affliction:
Your promise has given me life.
    Psalm 119:49–50

———

As a mother comforts her son, so I will comfort you,
and you will be comforted in Jerusalem.
    Isaiah 66:13

"Blessed are those who mourn, for they will be comforted."

 Matthew 5:4

———

Blessed be the God and Father of our Lord Jesus Christ, the Father of mercies and the God of all comfort. He comforts us in all our affliction, so that we may be able to comfort those who are in any kind of affliction, through the comfort we ourselves receive from God.

 2 Corinthians 1:3–4

Lord Jesus, Thank You for allowing me to cast my cares upon You. Lord, allow me to take the moments of comfort as they come. Allow me to acknowledge when those breezes come. Allow me to take comfort in the grace and love that You provide daily. Amen

CONTENTMENT

Serenity is often tied with nature. We think about the babble of a nearby stream, the chirping of various birds, the small crashes of incoming tides, and the faint whisper of the wind pushing through branches. We crave these sounds so much that we can find them in apps on our phones to help us relax. We do this to simulate peace, to simulate contentment. For some of us, that's the best we can get sometimes, but how amazing it is that God knew what these sounds would bring to our hearts.

*"So don't worry, saying, 'What will we eat?' or
'What will we drink?' or 'What will we wear?'
For the Gentiles eagerly seek all these things,
and your heavenly Father knows that you need
them. But seek first the kingdom of God and his
righteousness, and all these things will be provided
for you. Therefore don't worry about tomorrow,
because tomorrow will worry about itself. Each day
has enough trouble of its own."*

    Matthew 6:31–34

———

*But godliness with contentment is great gain. For
we brought nothing into the world, and we can take
nothing out. If we have food and clothing, we will
be content with these.*

    1 Timothy 6:6–8

He then told them, "Watch out and be on guard against all greed, because one's life is not in the abundance of his possessions."

Luke 12:15

———

I don't say this out of need, for I have learned to be content in whatever circumstances I find myself. I know both how to make do with little, and I know how to make do with a lot. In any and all circumstances I have learned the secret of being content—whether well fed or hungry, whether in abundance or in need.

Philippians 4:11–12

Father, I am content, and for that, I thank You. Father, there is so much chaos in this world, and yet You have taken the time to love me and put in me a content heart. Father, thank You for continually blessing me and allowing me to have moments of contentment. Drive me to share that contentment with others. Amen

Some of the most famous paintings in the world were inspired by nature. *Water Lilies* by Claude Monet, *The Starry Night* by Vincent Van Gogh, and *The Oxbow* by Thomas Cole are just to name a few. Books like *Call of the Wild* are often cited as the first books of avid readers, and most of us have heard songs that are dedicated to the scenery surrounding the artist. The point is that nature is often the building block of most people's creativity. God's creation is often what stirs the beginnings of our creations.

So God created man in his own image; he created him in the image of God; he created them male and female.

Genesis 1:27

———

I will praise you
because I have been remarkably and wondrously made.
Your works are wondrous,
and I know this very well.

Psalm 139:14

Do you see a person skilled in his work?
He will stand in the presence of kings.
He will not stand in the presence of the unknown.
Proverbs 22:29

———

All things were created through him, and apart
from him not one thing was created that has been
created.
John 1:3

———

For we are his workmanship, created in Christ Jesus
for good works, which God prepared ahead of time
for us to do.
Ephesians 2:10

Lord, God, I am amazed by Your creation. You have shown me Your creation every day and I am overwhelmed by its beauty. Father, never allow me to forget the beauty that You've created. Father, continue to inspire me so that I may glorify You through my creations. Amen

You'll rarely find a delight quite like children when they are outside. Whether they are climbing trees, catching fireflies, jumping in puddles, or simply playing tag, there is often a laughter that comes with children being in nature. From a young age, God provided us with the moments of delight that can only be provided by the outdoors.

How happy is the one who does not
walk in the advice of the wicked
or stand in the pathway with sinners
or sit in the company of mockers!
Instead, his delight is in the LORD's instruction,
and he meditates on it day and night.
He is like a tree planted beside flowing streams
that bears its fruit in its season
and whose leaf does not wither.
Whatever he does prospers.

    Psalm 1:1–3

———

If your instruction had not been my delight,
I would have died in my affliction.
I will never forget your precepts,
for you have given me life through them.

    Psalm 119:92–93

He brought me out to a spacious place;
he rescued me because he delighted in me.
    Psalm 18:19

————

Take delight in the LORD,
and he will give you your heart's desires.
    Psalm 37:4

————

"The LORD *your God is among you,*
a warrior who saves.
He will rejoice over you with gladness.
He will be quiet in his love.
He will delight in you with singing."
    Zephaniah 3:17

Father, You have continually provided for the moments of laughter and joy through Your creation. Lord, thank You for giving me the moments that have been the source of such joy. Father, I pray I never forget that it is You that has been the provider of delight. Allow me to use the joy that You have given and spread that to others. Amen

Devotion is something that is coupled with special attention and time. Ask any climber what they would accomplish if they could and they will tell you "Everest." Devotion is the only way to make it to the top. One must train the body, be financially prepared to even sign up, stock up on needed materials, and be mentally prepared to eventually make the nearly 70,000 foot journey. Some devote their lives to making this climb. This devotion, however, is nothing compared to the devoted love God has shown us through giving us His Son. How many of us can say we strive to have an Everest devotion to our Father in heaven?

This book of instruction must not depart from your mouth; you are to meditate on it day and night so that you may carefully observe everything written in it. For then you will prosper and succeed in whatever you do.

Joshua 1:8

———

"For where your treasure is, there your heart will be also."

Luke 12:34

"No servant can serve two masters, since either he will hate one and love the other, or he will be devoted to one and despise the other. You cannot serve both God and money."

 Luke 16:13

———

Be diligent to present yourself to God as one approved, a worker who doesn't need to be ashamed, correctly teaching the word of truth.

 2 Timothy 2:15

Father, thank You for giving us Your Son. The level of devotion You had to have for me is something I'll never understand. Father, I'm sorry. I have not lived a life of devotion to You. I have acted selfishly and put my relationship with You off to the side. Lord, instill in me a spirit that is devoted to chasing after You. Amen

It seems that every few years now, we hear about a forest fire in some part of the world. Most are started because of human error. There's a devastation that comes to the mind when we think about the loss that follows a forest fire. Something that gets lost in the chaos of the news is the encouragement that comes from rain. We bring in helicopters, fire trucks, and the military to help stop the fires, but there's nothing quite like rain in the forecast to calm the nerves of those trying to fight the fires.

The LORD is the one who will go before you. He will be with you; he will not leave you or abandon you. Do not be afraid or discouraged.

Deuteronomy 31:8

———

God is our refuge and strength,
a helper who is always found in times of trouble.

Psalm 46:1

———

"Aren't five sparrows sold for two pennies? Yet not one of them is forgotten in God's sight. Indeed, the hairs of your head are all counted. Don't be afraid; you are worth more than many sparrows."

Luke 12:6–7

"I have told you these things so that in me you may have peace. You will have suffering in this world. Be courageous! I have conquered the world."

    John 16:33

———

And let us watch out for one another to provoke love and good works, not neglecting to gather together, as some are in the habit of doing, but encouraging each other, and all the more as you see the day approaching.

    Hebrews 10:24–25

Heavenly Father, thank You for encouraging me. There is so much in this world that tries to bring me down, but there is joy that comes from knowing that You are God and that You will watch over me. Father, continue to watch over me. Protect me from the things in life that try to bring me down, and allow my spirit to be lifted, so that I may better serve You. Amen

We are constantly reminded that nothing on this earth will last forever. The seasons constantly show that there is a cycle of new life that ends, and new life forms again. One of the things that nature teaches us is that everything has a beginning and an end. It's because of these surroundings that we think it is something we are doomed to face as well, but there is a hope for eternal life, and that hope is found in Jesus Christ.

Before the mountains were born,
before you gave birth to the earth and the world,
from eternity to eternity, you are God.

    Psalm 90:2

———

He has made everything appropriate in its time. He
has also put eternity in their hearts, but no one can
discover the work God has done from beginning to
end.

    Ecclesiastes 3:11

———

This is eternal life: that they may know you, the
only true God, and the one you have sent—Jesus
Christ.

    John 17:3

"Truly I tell you, anyone who hears my word and believes him who sent me has eternal life and will not come under judgment but has passed from death to life."

   John 5:24

———

For the wages of sin is death, but the gift of God is eternal life in Christ Jesus our Lord.

   Romans 6:23

Lord Jesus, thank You for dying for me.
There are times that I fear death, but I know that
I have nothing to fear in You, Lord. Your death
is what brought eternal life. Your defeat of death
is what has given me victory in eternal life. Lord,
remind me daily that even though this world is
temporary, it is You that has proven time and
again that Your love is eternal. Amen

Most of us know families that have a camping trip once every couple of years, Maybe you're that friend or in that family. Something you'll often hear from these camping stories are the times spent around the fire. There's a comradery in camping. There's something about being outside with family that makes that time so much more special. This fellowship comes from removing the distractions of the world and allowing yourself to focus on each other.

Iron sharpens iron,
and one person sharpens another.
    Proverbs 27:17

———

Two are better than one because they have a good
reward for their efforts. For if either falls, his
companion can lift him up; but pity the one who
falls without another to lift him up.
    Ecclesiastes 4:9–10

———

Carry one another's burdens; in this way you will
fulfill the law of Christ.
    Galatians 6:2

Therefore encourage one another and build each
other up as you are already doing.
    1 Thessalonians 5:11

———

And let us watch out for one another to provoke love
and good works, not neglecting to gather together,
as some are in the habit of doing, but encouraging
each other, and all the more as you see the day
approaching.
    Hebrews 10:24–25

Father, I have allowed the distractions of the world to keep me from loving others. Instill in me a spirit that will allow me to focus on others. Put in me a heart that desires fellowship with others. Father, I know that I have allowed those relationships You put in my life to fall. Allow me to pick up those relationships and give the love You have given me to those around me. Amen

Like children learning to walk, birds learn to fly. Believe it or not, there are quite a few similarities between the two in this regard. Most have seen a child taking their early steps. They fall. They get back up. They fall again, but then something happens. Steps move from one or two to three or four. Hobbling becomes walking. Walking becomes running. The same goes for birds. They don't just start flying. When they fall, the parents do the same as us. They show grace and reinforce them for success. God is the same. As we learn to walk in faith with Him, we inevitably fall. This does not change the fact that He gives us grace so that we may succeed with Him in the future.

The law came along to multiply the trespass. But where sin multiplied, grace multiplied even more.
    Romans 5:20

———

For sin will not rule over you, because you are not under the law but under grace.
    Romans 6:14

———

Now if by grace, then it is not by works; otherwise grace ceases to be grace.
    Romans 11:6

But he said to me, "My grace is sufficient for you, for my power is perfected in weakness." Therefore, I will most gladly boast all the more about my weaknesses, so that Christ's power may reside in me.

2 Corinthians 12:9

———

For you are saved by grace through faith, and this is not from yourselves; it is God's gift—not from works, so that no one can boast.

Ephesians 2:8–9

Heavenly Father, thank You. Thank You for the times that I have tried to walk in this world without You. Father, every time that I try to do it on my own, I fall. Father, come alongside me so that I may not fall. Thank You for giving me grace when I have fallen. Thank You for giving me strength to stand and keep on walking. Amen

Happiness is frequently tied to nature. Small towns have festivals to celebrate the harvest season. Snowball fights and snowman sculptures seem only to add to the Christmas season. The spring shows children darting across yards hunting for multicolored eggs, and I'm fairly certain I've never seen anyone upset on the beach. The point is a fairly obvious one. Most can find happiness in nature in one form or another. Though it is often what we do in nature to gain happiness, it is the Creator that made the happiness possible through the creation of nature in the first place.

Therefore my heart is glad
and my whole being rejoices;
my body also rests securely.
   Psalm 16:9

———

Take delight in the LORD,
and he will give you your heart's desires.
   Psalm 37:4

———

A joyful heart makes a face cheerful,
but a sad heart produces a broken spirit.
   Proverbs 15:13

I know that there is nothing better for them than to rejoice and enjoy the good life.

    Ecclesiastes 3:12

———

Rejoice in the Lord always. I will say it again: Rejoice!

    Philippians 4:4

Lord, God, thank You for creating this world. There are so many things about what You have created that bring me joy. Father, allow me to continue to find joy in the things You've created. Allow me to constantly look out and see that what You have made is good and that it is in this goodness that I find happiness. Amen

Modern medicine seems to become more and more miraculous as science continues to prosper, and yet, most doctors will tell you the easiest way to stay healthy is to spend time outside. Being in nature is one of the best things a person can do for their health. You'll hear quite a few doctors say that the best thing someone can do is simply go for a walk for twenty minutes a day. The exercise helps, but so many doctors agree that the simple activity of being outside is what makes the difference.

My flesh and my heart may fail,
but God is the strength of my heart,
my portion forever.
    Psalm 73:26

———

He heals the brokenhearted
and bandages their wounds.
    Psalm 147:3

———

Don't be wise in your own eyes;
fear the LORD and turn away from evil.
This will be healing for your body
and strengthening for your bones.
    Proverbs 3:7–8

Don't you know that your body is a temple of the Holy Spirit who is in you, whom you have from God? You are not your own, for you were bought at a price. So glorify God with your body.

1 Corinthians 6:19–20

———

So, whether you eat or drink, or whatever you do, do everything for the glory of God.

1 Corinthians 10:31

Father, thank You for creating this world. Thank You for creating a nature that is so good for our bodies. Father, I pray that You continue to provide for my physical health, and put a spirit in me that drives to seek my spiritual health through You. Father, thank You again for giving me health. Allow me to use it to glorify You. Amen

HOPE

Some love the winter . . . others, not so much, but there's something about the time of year when the blooming starts. For those of us that hate the cold, the blooming often gives us a sense of hope. It means that the winter is ending, and new life and warmth are coming. There was a time when people thought that everything was over, but on the third day, the ultimate hope of mankind, He rose.

But those who trust in the LORD *will renew their strength; they will soar on wings like eagles; they will run and not become weary, they will walk and not faint.*

    Isaiah 40:31

———

I wait for the LORD*; I wait and put my hope in his word.*

    Psalm 130:5

———

Now may the God of hope fill you with all joy and peace as you believe so that you may overflow with hope by the power of the Holy Spirit.

    Romans 15:13

*We have also obtained access through him by faith
into this grace in which we stand, and we rejoice in
the hope of the glory of God. And not only that, but
we also rejoice in our afflictions, because we know
that affliction produces endurance, endurance
produces proven character, and proven character
produces hope.*

Romans 5:2–4

———

*Let us run with endurance the race that lies before
us, keeping our eyes on Jesus, the source and
perfecter of our faith. For the joy that lay before
him, he endured the cross, despising the shame,
and sat down at the right hand of the throne of God.
For consider him who endured such hostility from
sinners against himself, so that you won't grow
weary and give up.*

Hebrews 12:1–3

Lord, there is so much doubt in this world. There are so many things in this world that bring our spirits down. Father, remind me that there is hope in You. Allow me to know that whatever darkness may come, you are the light. Thank You for being the hope in my life, and allow me to know that it is You I put my hope in. Amen

Death Valley is a part of the largest desert in the United States. Though it is a vast, barren land, it is not the desert itself that makes this place interesting . . . it's the sky. There is so little light pollution in the area that at night, a camper can see an amount of stars that are not even visible in the smallest towns. Some who have seen this sky talk about how small this planet feels when they see how vast the night sky really is. It's a humbling experience . . . especially when we know that the almighty Creator that made those stars, took the time to make us as well.

Sitting down, he called the Twelve and said to them, "If anyone wants to be first, he must be last and servant of all."

    Mark 9:35

———

Live in harmony with one another. Do not be proud; instead, associate with the humble. Do not be wise in your own estimation.

    Romans 12:16

———

Do nothing out of selfish ambition or conceit, but in humility consider others as more important than yourselves.

    Philippians 2:3

Adopt the same attitude as that of Christ Jesus, who, existing in the form of God, did not consider equality with God as something to be exploited. Instead he emptied himself by assuming the form of a servant, taking on the likeness of humanity. And when he had come as a man, he humbled himself by becoming obedient to the point of death—even to death on a cross.

    Philippians 2:5–8

———

Who among you is wise and understanding? By his good conduct he should show that his works are done in the gentleness that comes from wisdom.

    James 3:13

Father, I am humbled by how amazingly You've made this world. There are so many things that I constantly look at and am just awestruck by what You've made. Father, forgive me. There are times that I do not act with humility. I act as if I am more than others around me. Father, teach me humility, and thank You for creating all the stars and still You love me. Amen

JOY

There's an old house on the banks of the Tennessee River. It's secluded, quiet, and an elderly couple has lived there for more than half a century. Outside of this house, overlooking the river, is a tree with a tire swing. Families will float by the house throughout the summer and stop by the swing once or twice a week. The rope has been replaced time and again, but when asked why by one of the families, the elderly husband simply said, "I can't replace the joy that comes from that swing . . . but I can at least replace a rope to keep that joy coming." When we know where that love comes from, joy is an outflow of that knowledge.

You reveal the path of life to me;
in your presence is abundant joy;
at your right hand are eternal pleasures.
   Psalm 16:11

———

This is the day the LORD has made;
let us rejoice and be glad in it.
   Psalm 118:24

*But the fruit of the Spirit is love, joy, peace,
patience, kindness, goodness, faithfulness,
gentleness, and self-control. The law is not against
such things.*

    Galatians 5:22–23

———

*"As the Father has loved me, I have also loved you.
Remain in my love. If you keep my commands
you will remain in my love, just as I have kept my
Father's commands and remain in his love. I have
told you these things so that my joy may be in you
and your joy may be complete."*

    John 15:9–11

Heavenly Father, You have taken such special care of me. You have provided me the moments in life that have been everything to me. There are so many moments of pure joy that I owe to You, Lord. Father, remind me that my joy only comes from the knowledge of Your love. Allow me to spread that joy to others, Lord. Amen

The scales of justice are always seeking balance.
Builders are often warned whenever they take
on new projects that involve uprooting trees.
The reason? The roots of the trees are what
keeps the ground stable. If the trees are taken
down, there have been instances of landslides.
Is this vengeance from the earth? No, of course
not. It is simply an effect of a cause. We must
remember the same in our lives; are we always
being punished by our wrongdoings? Not
necessarily. Sometimes these punishments are
simply effects to the actions we've chosen.

Pure and undefiled religion before God the Father is this: to look after orphans and widows in their distress and to keep oneself unstained from the world.

James 1:27

———

Isn't this the fast I choose: To break the chains of wickedness, to untie the ropes of the yoke, to set the oppressed free, and to tear off every yoke? Is it not to share your bread with the hungry, to bring the poor and homeless into your house, to clothe the naked when you see him, and not to ignore your own flesh and blood?

Isaiah 58:6–7

The LORD of Armies says this: "Make fair decisions.
Show faithful love and compassion to one another.
Do not oppress the widow or the fatherless, the
resident alien or the poor, and do not plot evil in
your hearts against one another."

    Zechariah 7:9–10

———

Don't be deceived: God is not mocked. For whatever
a person sows he will also reap,

    Galatians 6:7

———

Do not act unjustly when deciding a case. Do not
be partial to the poor or give preference to the rich;
judge your neighbor fairly.

    Leviticus 19:15

Father, I know that I have done wrong. Forgive me for when I have failed You. Lord, I know that the bad in my life is because of my choices and nothing else. Father, forgive me in the times that I have thought You were punishing me. God, allow me to move forward with perseverance so that I will not fail You again. Amen

There's nothing wrong with rest. Nature definitely provides that. Some might say the outdoors are better with a hammock, but there is a limit to rest. If one goes past that limit, they start entering a land of sloth. Nature is not really conducive to laziness. Nature is constantly changing. A breeze can be a precursor to a storm. The faint light from a sunrise can move to blistering heat. The welcomed crispness to winter air can be the first mark of a harsh winter. God shows with nature that there is a time for rest and a time for action. Take the moments of rest as they come, but be careful to not take the moment of rest as an opportunity for complacency.

The slacker craves, yet has nothing,
but the diligent is fully satisfied.
Proverbs 13:4

———

The one who is lazy in his work
is brother to a vandal.
Proverbs 18:9

Whatever you do, do it from the heart, as something done for the Lord and not for people, knowing that you will receive the reward of an inheritance from the Lord. You serve the Lord Christ.

   Colossians 3:23–24

———

In fact, when we were with you, this is what we commanded you: "If anyone isn't willing to work, he should not eat."

   2 Thessalonians 3:10

Holy Spirit, I have been lazy. I have taken a time of rest and moved past it. I struggle with a lazy spirit, Lord. Instill in me a spirit that drives to continue to work. Give me the discernment to know what is rest and what is complacent. Amen

One of the main rules given to most explorers and hikers is that no person should ever be alone. This is of course to keep us safe, but there are also a couple of things that come from following this rule: friendship and community. There's something that adds to being out in nature with those you care about. When you are with loved ones, the wonder of nature just becomes that much more special.

"My presence will go with you, and I will give you rest."

> *Exodus 33:14*

———

The LORD *is the one who will go before you. He will be with you; he will not leave you or abandon you. Do not be afraid or discouraged.*

> *Deuteronomy 31:8*

———

God provides homes for those who are deserted.
He leads out the prisoners to prosperity,
but the rebellious live in a scorched land.

> *Psalm 68:6*

He heals the brokenhearted
and bandages their wounds.
   Psalm 147:3

———

Blessed be the God and Father of our Lord Jesus
Christ, the Father of mercies and the God of all
comfort. He comforts us in all our affliction, so that
we may be able to comfort those who are in any
kind of affliction, through the comfort we ourselves
receive from God.
   2 Corinthians 1:3–4

Father, I feel so alone. I feel that no matter what it is that I do, I cannot escape this loneliness. Father, please put people in my life to fill the void in my life. Allow me to be able to have those that I can rely on and allow others to know that they can rely on me. Father, thank You for being with me always. I know that it is that knowledge that tells me that I am never alone. Amen

Every now and again, we hear about a proposal. If any of us have kept up with cultural trends, we rarely see a fancy restaurant proposal anymore. People prefer the seclusion of proposing outside at a special place, or they like making a place special so it's something they can look back at. There's permanence to the outdoors. A young man once proposed to his future bride in Colorado on a hike. He pointed to Mount Elbert and said, "As long as that mountain stands, I will love you." The most amazing thing about this is that God has loved us before the mountain ever was and will still love us after it's gone.

"But I say to you who listen: Love your enemies, do what is good to those who hate you, bless those who curse you, pray for those who mistreat you."
    Luke 6:27–28

———

Love is patient, love is kind. Love does not envy, is not boastful, is not arrogant, is not rude, is not self-seeking, is not irritable, and does not keep a record of wrongs.
    1 Corinthians 13:4–5

———

Above all, maintain constant love for one another, since love covers a multitude of sins.
    1 Peter 4:8

God's love was revealed among us in this way: God sent his one and only Son into the world so that we might live through him.

1 John 4:9

———

And we have come to know and to believe the love that God has for us. God is love, and the one who remains in love remains in God, and God remains in him.

1 John 4:16

*Heavenly Father, thank You for loving me.
Thank You for loving me enough to send
down your Son. Thank You for loving me in
times when I feel that I am unlovable. Thank You
for the love You continue to show me each day.
Father, thank You for loving me today, tomorrow,
and to the rest that may come. Amen*

MOTIVES

It seems these days that we always have to have a plan. Our world is so busy that it seems even something as simple as going outside has to have a motivation behind it. It's a reality that becomes more real the older we get. Seeking purpose is something that comes with everything we do. When we go out into nature, however, the motivations always seem to be positive. We go out for rest, to reconnect with family, to unplug from distraction; these are just to name a few. Whatever the reason, it's amazing to know that in the midst of God's creation, finding peace seems to be easier.

But the LORD said to Samuel, "Do not look at his appearance or his stature because I have rejected him. Humans do not see what the LORD sees, for humans see what is visible, but the LORD sees the heart."

1 Samuel 16:7

———

All a person's ways seem right to him,
but the LORD weighs hearts.

Proverbs 21:2

———

For am I now trying to persuade people, or God? Or am I striving to please people? If I were still trying to please people, I would not be a servant of Christ.

Galatians 1:10

Do nothing out of selfish ambition or conceit, but in humility consider others as more important than yourselves.

Philippians 2:3

———

Instead, just as we have been approved by God to be entrusted with the gospel, so we speak, not to please people, but rather God, who examines our hearts.

1 Thessalonians 2:4

Father, right now, I need direction. I need to know what my motivations are. I need to be able to focus on what is in front of me. Father, instill in me a desire to know why I do what I do. Father, give me motivation. Allow me to stand on my own feet and step forward, and allow my motives for doing anything to be centered around furthering Your Kingdom. Amen

PATIENCE

Ask any fisherman, and they will tell you that the secret to catching the perfect fish is found in one's patience. You sit in a boat. You cast your line and wait. Sometimes you'll get a couple of bites, but the real fisherman will wait for the perfect catch of the day. Patience is a virtue that so often goes overlooked in our world today, but God still shows us its worth, even through something as simple as a hook in the water.

The end of a matter is better than its beginning; a patient spirit is better than a proud spirit.

Ecclesiastes 7:8

———

Now if we hope for what we do not see, we eagerly wait for it with patience.

Romans 8:25

———

My dear brothers and sisters, understand this: Everyone should be quick to listen, slow to speak, and slow to anger, for human anger does not accomplish God's righteousness.

James 1:19–20

Therefore, brothers and sisters, be patient until the Lord's coming. See how the farmer waits for the precious fruit of the earth and is patient with it until it receives the early and the late rains. You also must be patient. Strengthen your hearts, because the Lord's coming is near.

James 5:7–8

———

The Lord does not delay his promise, as some understand delay, but is patient with you, not wanting any to perish but all to come to repentance.

2 Peter 3:9

Lord, I know that I have struggled with patience. There is so much in this world that I just want now. Father, I know it is wrong but I have a spirit that refuses to wait. Calm that spirit, Lord, and instill in me a patient heart so that I may wait on the things that You would have for me. Amen

It's interesting, the things we work for in this world. Children go to school for twelve years to receive a high school diploma, and can barely tell you what it looks like outside of their name being on it. Some of us will put hours of work into buying a car just to sell it a few years later. Our perseverance normally is expended on the fleeting, but ask any climber about getting to the top of a mountain . . . the view never changes. God's creation is constant.

And not only that, but we also rejoice in our
afflictions, because we know that affliction
produces endurance, endurance produces proven
character, and proven character produces hope. This
hope will not disappoint us, because God's love
has been poured out in our hearts through the Holy
Spirit who was given to us.

    Romans 5:3–5

———

Let us not get tired of doing good, for we will reap at
the proper time if we don't give up.

    Galatians 6:9

Therefore, since we also have such a large cloud of witnesses surrounding us, let us lay aside every hindrance and the sin that so easily ensnares us. Let us run with endurance the race that lies before us, keeping our eyes on Jesus, the source and perfecter of our faith. For the joy that lay before him, he endured the cross, despising the shame, and sat down at the right hand of the throne of God.

Hebrews 12:1–2

———

Consider it a great joy, my brothers and sisters, whenever you experience various trials, because you know that the testing of your faith produces endurance. And let endurance have its full effect, so that you may be mature and complete, lacking nothing.

James 1:2–4

Father, I have been guilty of working for the things that do not satisfy. I put hours into work that never satisfies. I chase money that is never enough. Father, I know that working hard is not bad, but give me the perseverance to work hard for You and Your kingdom. Father, fix my eyes upon You so that I may work toward You each and every day. Amen

Praising God is one of the most important things we are called to do. Worship is imperative to have a relationship with God. Something I often hear about church camps when training their staff is that they will talk about a morning hike during their training. This morning hike will often end with being in an open area, watching the sunrise, and worshipping. Being out in what God's created is one of the easiest ways to be closer to Him.

I will praise God's name with song
and exalt him with thanksgiving.
　　Psalm 69:30

―――――

Hallelujah!
Praise God in his sanctuary.
Praise him in his mighty expanse.
Praise him for his powerful acts;
praise him for his abundant greatness.
　　Psalm 150:1–2

For from him and through him and to him are all things. To him be the glory forever. Amen.

    Romans 11:36

———

Now to him who is able to protect you from stumbling and to make you stand in the presence of his glory, without blemish and with great joy, to the only God our Savior, through Jesus Christ our Lord, be glory, majesty, power, and authority before all time, now and forever. Amen.

    Jude 24–25

Father, You are an awesome God. You have created the stars, the sky, the mountains, the oceans, the rivers, the grass, and the dirt. Father, You have created things so big that I can't comprehend them, and You have created things so small that I never notice them. You are the all powerful, all knowing God, and You love me. Thank You, Father. Thank You for all of the amazing things You do. Amen

There's a marine biologist that lives in southern Alabama on a tiny island. Part of his morning ritual is to wake up every morning and walk down to the beach for his quiet time. He prays every morning for thirty minutes and then reads his Bible. After an hour he goes back home and has breakfast with his family. When asked about why he prays there every morning, he points to the waves and says, "The crashing of those waves have always been there. That sound has been the most constant thing in my life, and it doesn't even compare to the constant love God has for me . . . the sound is a reminder that I am loved."

"Whenever you pray, you must not be like the hypocrites, because they love to pray standing in the synagogues and on the street corners to be seen by people. . . . But when you pray, go into your private room, shut your door, and pray to your Father who is in secret. And your Father who sees in secret will reward you. When you pray, don't babble like the Gentiles, since they imagine they'll be heard for their many words. . . .

"Therefore, you should pray like this: Our Father in heaven, your name be honored as holy. Your kingdom come. Your will be done on earth as it is in heaven. Give us today our daily bread. And forgive us our debts, as we also have forgiven our debtors. And do not bring us into temptation, but deliver us from the evil one.

"For if you forgive others their offenses, your heavenly Father will forgive you as well. But if you don't forgive others, your Father will not forgive your offenses."

Matthew 6:5–15

*If you remain in me and my words remain in you,
ask whatever you want and it will be done for you.*
   John 15:7

———

*In the same way the Spirit also helps us in our
weakness, because we do not know what to pray for
as we should, but the Spirit himself intercedes for
us with unspoken groanings.*
   Romans 8:26

———

*Don't worry about anything, but in everything,
through prayer and petition with thanksgiving,
present your requests to God.*
   Philippians 4:6

Lord, I know I do not pray nearly as much as I need to. I know that I put off time with You, when it should be the first thing I do every day. Father, forgive me for not spending as much time with You as I should. Allow me to wake up and know that it is You I should start my day with. Amen

One of the first things a person is told to do if they ever find themselves lost in the woods is to stay put and build a shelter. Most people don't know that with a little knowledge, God has provided all the protection a person can need. If someone has some heavy sticks and some leaves, they can build a strong enough shelter that will protect them from the elements. It's interesting to think that God can use a few sticks that keep us safe enough from whatever the world may throw at us.

Protect me as the pupil of your eye;
hide me in the shadow of your wings.

  Psalm 17:8

——————

*The angel of the L*ORD *encamps*
around those who fear him, and rescues them.

  Psalm 34:7

——————

The mountains surround Jerusalem
*and the L*ORD *surrounds his people,*
both now and forever.

  Psalm 125:2

The name of the LORD is a strong tower;
the righteous run to it and are protected.
    Proverbs 18:10

———

But the Lord is faithful; he will strengthen and
guard you from the evil one.
    2 Thessalonians 3:3

Heavenly Father, this world feels so overwhelming sometimes. I know that I am to cast my cares upon You. Lord, allow me to know that whatever this world may throw at me, I can reach out to You for protection. Father, allow me to constantly know that whatever may come . . . I have You, and You have never been defeated. Amen

Everyone knows a "lawn guy." Most of us have seen a man that takes meticulous care to make sure that his lawn is in tip-top condition. One of the things I've heard screamed by one of them is "What is the point of weeds!?" This gentleman would angrily rip these nuisances from his lawn until he decided to have this question answered by a florist that attended his church. He came to find out that weeds actually build and protect the soil. The man still hates weeds, but he doesn't rush out to exorcise the yard of a single dandelion when he sees one. How many of us have misunderstood a purpose God has for us?

When all has been heard, the conclusion of the matter is this: fear God and keep his commands, because this is for all humanity.

    Ecclesiastes 12:13

———

"My Father is glorified by this: that you produce much fruit and prove to be my disciples."

    John 15:8

———

But I consider my life of no value to myself; my purpose is to finish my course and the ministry I received from the Lord Jesus, to testify to the gospel of God's grace.

    Acts 20:24

He has saved us and called us with a holy calling, not according to our works, but according to his own purpose and grace, which was given to us in Christ Jesus before time began.

2 Timothy 1:9

———

Sing to him; sing praise to him; tell about all his wondrous works! Honor his holy name; let the hearts of those who seek the LORD rejoice.

1 Chronicles 16:9–10

Lord Jesus, I know that there is a purpose in my life that I'm choosing not to live up to. I know that there is a plan that You have for me, and I am not living up to that plan. Father, I worry that I will not be able to live up to whatever You've called me to be. Allow me to move forward in knowing that You are a great God, and that whatever good I do, is because You work through me. Amen

Seeking the right foundation is everything in construction. If you go to the ocean, you'll find a few houses that are on stilts, hovering over the sands. We all know that building on sand is not exactly a wise decision, so how do they do it? They dig down into the sand to place the stilts into an area that is as hard as rock. This anchors the stilts—providing the kind of stability needed to keep the house in place. Like the houses, our souls also need an anchor. That anchor should be in Christ.

I always let the L<small>ORD</small> guide me.
Because he is at my right hand,
I will not be shaken.
  Psalm 16:8

———

He brought me up from a desolate pit,
out of the muddy clay,
and set my feet on a rock,
making my steps secure.
  Psalm 40:2

*The person who trusts in the L*ORD*, whose confidence indeed is the L*ORD*, is blessed. He will be like a tree planted by water: it sends its roots out toward a stream, it doesn't fear when heat comes, and its foliage remains green. It will not worry in a year of drought or cease producing fruit.*

Jeremiah 17:7–8

———

Therefore, since we are receiving a kingdom that cannot be shaken, let us be thankful. By it, we may serve God acceptably, with reverence and awe, for our God is a consuming fire.

Hebrews 12:28–29

Father, this world is rocky. I feel like I am being tossed around this world without any sense of stability. Lord, I know that it is through You that I find that stability. Allow me to trust in You. I know that it is something I struggle with, but I also know that it is only from Your foundation that I can build from. Amen

Some have a natural green thumb. Some not so much. We all learned who the gardeners were in elementary school when we tried to have seeds take root in a Styrofoam cup. Those of us that continued gardening or farming probably know of a time when water was so hard to find that we would water our plants twice in a day, but nevertheless, there's a thankfulness among green thumbs when prayers are answered with rain. It's a thankfulness most scratch their heads at but is understood by all that know the importance of a simple rainstorm.

Give thanks to the LORD, for he is good;
his faithful love endures forever.
    Psalm 118:1

————

For we know that the one who raised the Lord Jesus
will also raise us with Jesus and present us with
you. Indeed, everything is for your benefit so that, as
grace extends through more and more people, it may
cause thanksgiving to increase to the glory of God.
    2 Corinthians 4:14–15

————

Rejoice always, pray constantly, give thanks in
everything; for this is God's will for you in Christ
Jesus.
    1 Thessalonians 5:16–18

Let the word of Christ dwell richly among you, in all wisdom teaching and admonishing one another through psalms, hymns, and spiritual songs, singing to God with gratitude in your hearts.

    Colossians 3:16

———

Every good and perfect gift is from above, coming down from the Father of lights, who does not change like shifting shadows.

    James 1:17

Father, I am so thankful for the things that You do in my life. I know that there are so many things that You have done that have gone unnoticed. Father, I pray that all that You do is something that I do take notice in. Allow me to count my blessings so that I may grow even stronger in my thankfulness of You. Amen

Christmas tree farming is difficult. The process takes the majority of the year and a person has to dedicate four years of work before there is any pay off in the work that has been done. The first step is to tie a seedling to a stick of bamboo to make sure that the growth of the tree will be as straight as possible. Then, you wiggle a flat shovel into the earth, place the bamboo into the ground, and close it. Once it's grows, you trim it with a machete to make sure it grows into a cone like shape. This is repeated until the trees are ready to be sold at Christmas. This kind of work requires a lot of faith and patience. A farmer has to live by a plan in order to have success. In our walks today, do we live by a plan that will yield success for His kingdom?

Commit your activities to the L*ORD*,
and your plans will be established.
    Proverbs 16:3

———

Do everything in love.
    1 Corinthians 16:14

———

And God is able to make every grace overflow to
you, so that in every way, always having everything
you need, you may excel in every good work.
    2 Corinthians 9:8

Whatever you do, do it from the heart, as something done for the Lord and not for people, knowing that you will receive the reward of an inheritance from the Lord. You serve the Lord Christ.

   Colossians 3:23–24

———

Come now, you who say, "Today or tomorrow we will travel to such and such a city and spend a year there and do business and make a profit." Yet you do not know what tomorrow will bring—what your life will be! For you are like vapor that appears for a little while, then vanishes. Instead, you should say, "If the Lord wills, we will live and do this or that."

   James 4:13–15

Heavenly Father, I feel that the work I'm doing is pointless. I feel that there are so many tedious things that are keeping me from enjoying what I do. Father, teach me to know that the work I do has a purpose; and if it doesn't, allow me to find the kind of work that does have purpose. Father, give me the drive to work hard, and allow my work to glorify You. Amen